THE ESSENTIAL

BM

Z4

E85 Roadster and E86 Coupé including M and Alpina

2003 to 2009

Your marque expert:
David Smitheram

VELOCE PUBLISHING
THE PUBLISHER OF FINE AUTOMOTIVE BOOKS

www.veloce.co.uk

First published in June 2018 by Veloce Publishing Limited, Veloce House, Parkway Farm Business Park, Middle Farm Way,
Poundbury, Dorchester, Dorset, DT1 3AR, England.
Telephone 01305 260068/Fax 01305 250479/email info@veloce.co.uk/web www.veloce.co.uk or www.velocebooks.com.
ISBN: 978-1-787111-96-7 UPC: 6-36847-01196-3

Introduction
– the purpose of this book

This book guides you through the choosing and buying process, helping you select the best BMW Z4 for your budget and pointing out potential problem areas along the way.

Considering the performance of my own Z4M Roadster, and given that I have used it for everything from commuting, continental road trips and track days, the running costs have been exceptionally low. Reliability has been everything I would expect from a BMW. In fact, when writing this book I had to research potential problems from many sources, as my own car has been virtually trouble free.

Z3M Coupé and Z4M Roadster at the Nürburgring.

Background

Following the commercially successful Z3, the Z4 was designed as an all-new two-seater Roadster with true sports car aspirations. Production started in 2002 in Spartanburg, South Carolina with the first models ready for delivery to US showrooms in late 2002, and worldwide in early to mid 2003. The 'flame surfaced' styling by Anders Warming and team, overseen by Chris Bangle, was distinctive, even controversial, but it has aged well, proving its contemporary styling.

Eye-catching M Coupé.

The wider, ultra-rigid bodyshell and chassis was more than twice as stiff as the Z3 Roadster. Modern, multi-link rear suspension matched with smooth, powerful engines meant the 'E85' Z4 Roadster had all the ingredients needed to produce a great sports car. It was perhaps inevitable that even higher performance versions would follow, with Alpina releasing the range-topping Roadster S 3.4 in 2004, and later in 2006 the ultra high performance M derivatives were produced.

Eye-catching E86 Coupés

Motorsport Coupé in action at Brands Hatch.

completed the line-up in 2006. The ready to race Motorsport Coupé proved to be a race winner on the international stage.

With much of the suspension, engine range and transmission being shared with the E46 3 Series model range, the Z4 mechanicals are well proven, which should mean that spares remain available for decades to come.

The all-new E89 Z4 model was launched in 2009. These are completely different cars aimed at a different type of buyer, and therefore are not covered by this guide.

Road tests

The press appeared confused regarding the market BMW was aiming its new Z4 at, with some publications offering glowing reports, whilst others rated aspects of the cars as merely above average.

Evo magazine gave the 3-litre Roadster four out of five stars, complimenting the 'terrific engine,' with the later Z4M Roadster and Coupé receiving four and a half stars, being described as "Exhilarating and characterful," and losing just half a star for stiff suspension.

Road and Track rated the 3-litre Roadster highly, but said the engine felt "underpowered and the suspension is tuned too softly for hard driving."

Buyers, on the other hand, almost universally loved the Z4.

Exhilarating and characterful.

Values

History may come to view the Z4 E85 Roadster and E86 Coupé as the sweet spot in terms of BMW sports car production, where the blend of technology, corrosion resistance, driving dynamics, manual gearboxes and normally-aspirated engines were at their very best. With just under 200,000 cars produced worldwide for supply on all continents, there is a good choice of cars on the used market, allowing a buyer to find a specification that suits them.

There were few criticisms of the car, but those that were picked up consistently in reviews, such as improving the firm ride, are covered later in this guide. Those models produced in smaller numbers such as the Alpina S, M Roadster and M Coupé, as well as the 3-litre Si Coupé, have begun to rise in value, with all other models appearing to have halted their depreciation, making now a good time to buy.

Values have begun to rise for some models.

Contents

THE ESSENTIAL BUYER'S GUIDE™ CURRENCY
At the time of publication a BG unit of currency "●" equals approximately
£1.00/US$1.34/Euro 1.13. Please adjust to suit current exchange rates using
Sterling as the base currency.

1 Is it the right car for you?
– marriage guidance

The Z4 is a great all-rounder, with enough comfort, reliability and practicality to be used every day or kept for weekend thrills. Whilst they shouldn't be regarded as low maintenance or fault-free, the quality of the parts used by BMW and strong mechanicals mean that ownership is frequently trouble-free.

Roadster or Coupé?

Roadster or Coupé?
Your first choice will be between the E85 Roadster with its electrically operated soft top, or the E86 Coupé (fixed metal roof). The Roadster was also available with an optional, removable hard top offering additional security and weather protection. Thought needs to be given to removal (it's a two-person job) and storage when not in use. Depending on condition and colour these change hands for around ●900 on the used market.

   The Roadster has that wonderful open air feeling allowing you to hear the glorious engine note and appreciate the sun on your face, whilst the Coupé is rarer, with more storage space and arguably a more sleek appearance.

Engines
The smallest engine is a 2-litre four-cylinder, producing 148bhp, then there are the six-cylinder engines in various sizes and power outputs: 2.2-litre (168bhp), 2.5-litre (177bhp to 215bhp), 3-litre (215bhp to 261bhp), 3.4-litre Alpina Roadster S (300bhp) and 3.2-litre M (330bhp to 338bhp). The exact power output depended on the country in which the model was sold, and the production date of the Z4.

Optional Roadster hardtop.

   All engines give strong performance, with the straight six engines adding smoothness and a pleasing aural note. Automatic and semi automatic gearboxes were available on 2.2-, 2.5- and 3-litre engines.

Pre-face-lift front light.

Face-lift front light.

Face-lift
In 2006 came a mid-life face-lift, most easily spotted by the fitting of different front and rear lights, together with subtle styling changes to the front and rear bumpers, plus some new engines and gearboxes were introduced. In addition the Coupé and M models were launched.

Pre-face-lift rear light.   Face-lift rear light.

Fuel

No diesel models were produced, with all engines running on unleaded petrol. Higher performance engines will benefit from premium, high octane petrol, particularly the M models.

Driver fit and comfort

A wide range of seat and steering column adjustment allows for a generous variety of driver proportions.

Seating is low, but the sills are easy to get across. Access to Roadsters is, of course, even easier with the roof down.

Drivers or passengers beyond 1880mm (74 inches) in height may struggle for head or leg room, but much will depend on their exact proportions.

Seats can be manual or electric, with electric seats also having three memory settings – useful if multiple drivers share the car. Standard sports seats are comfortable but lack lateral support when the car is driven through corners. M Sports, Alpina and M seats are more desirable to many, offering a more enclosedt, sporty feel.

The steering column adjusts manually, for height and reach.

Z4s are quiet cars, with normal conversation possible even with the Roadster's roof lowered at motorway speeds.

All Z4s except M and Alpina models have run-flat tyres, providing a degree of reassurance that, in the event of a puncture, the journey can be completed at a reduced speed. M models have an inflation fluid and compressor that can repair small holes in their conventional tyres.

Seat belt height is non-adjustable.

The Roadster electric roof should retract quickly and smoothly.

Roof

The Roadster's electric roof is fully automatic on all models (except the most basic 2-litre in non SE or Sport trim); it just requires a press and hold of a dashboard button, no need to release any clips by hand. At the time of launch, it boasted the world's fastest retraction time of ten seconds. The roof is very reliable in everyday use, and, being multi-layered fabric, is easy to care for.

The Coupé has a fixed roof. A sunroof was not an option, although the 'double bubble' roof skin is attractive, an aerodynamic aid, and offers fractionally increased headroom.

Space

Compared with a modern saloon or SUV, the Z4 feels more compact inside, but this should be seen as part of the appeal: you sit *in* the car, not *on* it.

A small glove box, shallow door pockets, and a drop-down door between the seats can be used for keeping small items out of sight.

The Roadster boot (trunk) is well sized for a two-seater, its 260 litres giving enough room for two small cases. The boot volume reduces by just 20 litres when the roof is down.

The Coupé boot is large for a two-seat sports car, at 340 litres with the roll out luggage cover open.

Both the M Coupé and M Roadster have their battery relocated to the right corner of the boot, due to the twin exhaust boxes taking up the space under the boot carpet – the location usually used by all other Z4 models. This does slightly reduce the M model's storage volume by around 40 litres.

Perhaps surprisingly, the Z4 did not come with a place to support a drink, unless fitted with the optional slide out cup holder(s) located underneath the air vents on the left and right of the car. However, these can be retro-fitted. Coupés have a holder for sunglasses above the centre mirror.

M Roadster boot with battery in corner.

The Coupé has great boot space.

Slide out cup holder.

Running costs

Thanks to well proven mechanicals and the high quality of OEM parts, these can be cost-effective cars to run. Fuel economy is respectable for a performance car, especially when driven on longer journeys on main roads – similar, if not better than an average saloon car. Thanks to excellent access to the spacious engine bay, common service tasks such as oil and filter or spark plug changes are simple for the average home mechanic. You can also replace front or rear light bulbs with ease; front bulbs are accessed through an access flap in the wheelarch, with a coin the only tool needed.

With a four-star NCAP safety rating (the highest rating for a convertible at the time of launch) and decent standard fit security features, the cost of insurance is very reasonable.

One of the largest running costs for any car is depreciation. If you buy wisely and look after your BMW, you may find you break even when it's time to sell, possibly even selling for more than you paid, if you are fortunate.

Will a Z4 fit in my garage?

Although not a big car, some small garages may struggle to accommodate it; see chapter 17 for dimensions. Rear parking sensors (PDC) and electric folding mirrors were an option, and may help in some situations.

PDC rear parking sensors.

Any minus points?

You sit towards the rear of the car looking forwards over a long bonnet; this can make pulling out of a junction between parked cars difficult.

Kerbs and speed bumps can cause the bumper or undertray to catch on the underside. This is more noticeable if the car has been lowered on aftermarket springs.

Rivals

The Z4 Roadster with its sporty ambitions was pitched in magazine group tests against the Audi TT,

Power folding mirrors.

Class rival AMG SLK is automatic only.

The Corvette C6 could be seen as an unusual rival to the Z4.

Mercedes SLK, Honda S2000 and particularly the Porsche Boxster. The Z4 Coupé that was designed and produced later was regularly compared with the Porsche Cayman.

Opinions vary as to whether the Porsche models were 'better' than the Z4, with personal preference coming down to price, use and image as much as anything else. Both Porsche models have suffered with well-publicised engine issues, and with the engine located just behind the cockpit, certain maintenance tasks are more difficult.

2 Cost considerations
– affordable, or a money pit?

Servicing

Servicing is calculated by time or by using the on-board computer that counts down how many miles (petrol used) until the next service. The maximum time between services is 24 months, or 15,550 miles (25,000km).

Servicing follows this order: oil service, inspection 1, oil service, inspection 2, then back to the start.

M models also follow the same order, with one exception; they receive a 1200-mile running-in service at a dealership where the gearbox, differential and engine oils are changed. Internet opinion sometimes suggests that the M engines were first filled with running-in oils but this has been proved not to be the case; they were factory filled with the same oils that are used at the dealerships.

Reliable on road and track.
(Courtesy Xtreme Sports Photography)

Different countries have slightly different service recommendations. Certain models also have different service requirements, so check the service book for an accurate description.

Oil services, as the name suggests, are when the engine oil and filter are changed, together with various checks.

Depending on model, the inspection 1 service usually involves changing the cabin filter, brake fluid (or every two years) and many other checks. Inspection 2 adds to this by replacing the air filter, the gearbox and diff oils, and more. Spark plugs are changed at 100k miles, or at inspection 2. Cam chains are fitted to all engines, so there are no expensive cambelt changes to worry about.

The inspection services on M models are more expensive than all other Z4s, as their high revving S54 engine requires valve clearances to be checked and adjusted, ideally with a printout of the values.

Changing M shims at an inspection service.

Oil is the lifeblood of a car, and it is this author's recommendation that the oil and oil filter be changed more regularly then BMW suggests, prolonging the life of these generally strong and reliable engines.

Servicing may have been carried out by a main dealership, independent BMW specialist, local garage, or the owner. Whichever servicing method is chosen, the same rules apply. Make sure the services are carried out on time or earlier, with invoices, receipts or dealer stamps kept, and that quality parts are used. Most common jobs such as servicing, brakes and suspension work are well within the reach of the average home mechanic, working without a ramp or lift.

Z4s have a multitude of clever electronic sensors with multiplex/canbus wiring, and, far from something to be nervous of, this actually makes diagnosing issues much easier by plugging a device into the OBD2 (Onboard Diagnostic) socket, located just above the driver's shins.

Regular servicing is recommended.

Changing from run-flats to conventional tyres improves the ride.

Tyres
The right tyres, correctly inflated, help keep you safe, and greatly enhance the handling and performance of these fabulous cars. They also have a direct bearing on the comfort and ride. One of the main criticisms of the Z4 when new was the harsh ride, at least part of which can be attributed to early types of run-flat tyres that were fitted as standard to all models except Alpina and M. If you are buying a car that still runs on its original run-flat tyres, consider changing them to a more modern design, or switching to conventional tyres with a noticeable improvement in weight, price and comfort.

Spare parts
Availability of spare parts is excellent, both from BMW main dealers and a host of independent sellers.

A useful resource is www.realoem.com, which provides the exact same exploded diagrams and part numbers as your BMW main dealer.

Insurance
This will vary hugely depending on an individual's age, address and risk, but an 'average' owner should be pleasantly surprised when receiving a quote.

Fuel
Z4s were only available with petrol engines, with average realistic fuel economy varying between 25 and 40mpg depending on the engine and usage, with the higher figures easily

Insurance cost is good for a sports car.

achievable on longer motorway journeys, or for those with a lighter right foot. The 2.2-, 2.5- and 3-litre six-cylinder engines give a broadly similar fuel economy, with just a few mpg difference.

Decent fuel economy, considering the performance.

Optional Roadster rear spoiler is still available from BMW dealers.

3 Living with a BMW Z4
– will you get along together?

The BMW Z4 is a near ideal blend of modern convenience, safety and reliability, together with the typical pleasure of a front-engined, rear-wheel drive sports car. They are not overly complicated for first-time users. Safety handling systems are there to assist and keep you safe, but can be switched off if desired.

Simple interior design.

Handling
BMW did a great job in this area, but, as the magazine quotes in the introduction show, you can never please everyone. The good news is that BMW created a predictable, neutral-handling Roadster and Coupé, with incredibly efficient traction and stability control systems. If you want a livelier machine, it is happy to oblige – one press of the DSC/ DTC button allows a certain amount of wheelslip, while a long press turns off the handling and wheelspin assistance, but leaves the anti-lock braking fully functional.

Z4s are great-handling cars.
(Courtesy Elizabeth Smitheram)

For those who want a more focused ride, either for comfort or better handling, this can be achieved through geometry setup changes, different tyres, or aftermarket spring and shock absorber replacements.

Removing the factory pin allows extra front negative camber.

Performance
Every petrol engine fitted to the Z4 is modern, smooth and powerful. Even the smallest 2-litre, four-cylinder engine delivers a 0-60 time of 8.2 seconds, and a top speed of 137mph. The fire-breathing M models deliver sub 5-second 0-60 times, and easily reach their limited 155mph top speed. The 55-litre fuel tank results in a typical range of 250 to 350 miles of driving, but less or more is certainly possible. The five-speed gearbox fitted to the pre-face-lift 2.2- and 2.5-litre cars has a slightly shorter top gear, making it a fraction noisier, and it uses more fuel at higher cruising speeds. All other models were fitted with a six-speed manual gearbox, with well-spaced ratios and a long sixth gear for relaxed long distance cruising.

The six-speed SSG (also known as SMG) semi-automatic gearbox in pre-face-lift 2.5- and 3-litre cars gives similar performance, responsiveness and fuel economy to the manual, but is perhaps an acquired taste. The five- and later six-speed torque converting automatic 'Steptronic' models are only slightly slower through the gears than their manual equivalents.

SSG semi-automatic gearbox.

Paddle shift automatic on sports steering wheel.

The six-cylinder engines give a great balance between torque at low and middle revs and top end power, which is what most drivers would want from a practical sports car.

Owners report that the 2.2- (168bhp) and 2.5- (192bhp and 215bhp) litre engines are particularly enjoyable to use on minor roads, when these shorter stroke engines rev freely.

The later 2.5- and 3-litre Si engines fitted in the post 2006 models gained more power, 215bhp and 261bhp respectively, while the standard 2.5 dropped to 177bhp with remapping and induction changes.

The 295bhp 3.4-litre engine fitted in the Alpina Roadster S is especially strong in the middle of its rev range, and is slightly more relaxed in its delivery compared to the high revving but ultimately more powerful M versions.

The 3.2-litre S54 M engine comes straight from the M3 model, and produces around 330bhp in US markets where extra catalytic convertors are fitted, and 338bhp in Europe (343bhp by British unit measurement). The M models deliver incredible performance, with independent road tests recording 0-60 times of 4.7 seconds. Revving to 8000rpm, they deliver maximum power at 7900rpm, so don't be afraid to hang onto that gear when overtaking – the engine is designed to be driven hard once the oil has warmed up.

M54 3-litre sound generator.

A key feature of any sports car is the way it sounds, and a BMW straight six has a distinctive and pleasing tone. The 3-litre was fitted with a sound generator that channelled a small part of the induction noise to the cabin. This can be retrofitted to the 2.2- and 2.5-litre cars, and can be made louder by removing sound deadening foam inserts. Exhaust back boxes can be modified, or switched with sports replacements for more aural drama, but be aware that some can introduce a tiring drone to the cabin at low revs.

Lights
Halogen front lights are merely adequate, and can be improved upon by fitting brighter, modern bulbs. Those models with Xenon (High Intensity Discharge) lights are excellent, in brightness and spread of light. You can

A height adjustment wheel means Halogen headlights.

No height adjustment wheel means the car has Xenon headlights.

Side indicators hidden behind BMW badges.

Extended leather roll hoops are strong.

tell if the car has Halogen or Xenon lights by the presence of a headlight level adjustment wheel by the light switch. If it has one, the car has Halogen.

Rear lights on post 2006 cars changed to LED light bars housed in a different looking cluster, with a clear centre brakelight on Roadsters. The side indicators are distinctive, partly hidden behind the BMW badge on the front wings.

Sensibly, all Z4s had twin reversing lamps, which were useful at night.

Visibility

With height adjustment as standard on both driver and passenger seats, it should be possible for most occupants to find a height from which they can see clearly through the large windscreen. The rear windows are heated glass as standard, considerably better than some rivals (early S2000 and Boxster) which still had flexible plastic windows. Wing mirrors are permanently heated, so condensation is never a problem in cold climates. All cars have air-conditioning or climate control as standard; both are useful in the winter to quickly clear misted windows.

Safety

Z4s achieved a four-star Euro NCAP rating – the highest result among cars of its time when launched. Airbags are fitted to protect occupants from the front and side, with ABS and traction/stability control as standard. Strong brakes, a wide stance and low centre of gravity give reassuring handling. Should the worst happen, the bodyshell is strong, with collapsible components designed to absorb energy.

A traditionally poor aspect of safety in soft top cars is what happens in the event of a roll-over situation. To address this, the designers combined high tensile steels into the windscreen surround and roll-over hoops behind the seats, and thoroughly roll tested it.

4 Relative values
– which model for you?

Most cars appear to be at the bottom of their depreciation curve now, with some models starting to appreciate. Value and demand are seasonal for all sports cars, but especially so for the Roadsters, for which spring and summer seems to be the time when buyers wake up to the appeal of something fun in the sun.

The newest, low mileage, well-equipped cars with full history command the highest asking price. Those made in the lowest numbers, such as M, Alpina, 3.0 Si and Coupé models, are especially desirable.

Desirable Z4M Coupé model.

Equipment levels
BMW expects most buyers to customise their new car to a certain degree when they first order from the showroom. This adds to the difficulty when it comes to valuation, since working out what equipment was standard and what was optional on a given model is complicated.

M models came in one main trim level with the exception of the US-only Premium Package, which put together cruise control, upgraded audio and

Supportive sports seat.

more. Alpina offered the popular Lux pack incorporating Xenon lights, cruise control, sat nav, a CD multi-changer, wind deflector and more.

Other models were available in Base, SE or Sport trim. Differences included suspension (sport was firmer) and seat changes (M sports had more supportive, hugging bolsters and bases) as well as alloy wheel design and size to name a few.

Many sellers mistakenly list standard equipment in adverts as if it were an optional extra. An online search may help you work out what was standard and was an option for that particular model and year. Also, ordering BMW sales brochures from an auction site like eBay can help immensely.

Genuine BMW retrofit kits are available for heated seats, PDC, sat nav, Bluetooth and more. Pre-face-lift cars were usually fitted with all wiring in place making the installation of items like heated memory seats much easier. Post 2006 face-lift cars were only fitted with wiring for the options selected when new.

Some aftermarket modifications like uprated brakes, quality suspension, stubby aerial, genuine CSL alloy wheels, performance exhausts, and, in the case of M models, carbon airboxes or induction kits, may increase desirability for some, but not necessarily price.

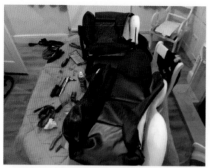
Retrofitting heated seat elements.

Optional Cruise Control can be retrofitted.

Popular 19in CSL wheels.

Stubby aftermarket aerials are popular.

Anything likely to reduce values?

There is no certainty that any single feature will reduce the value of a Z4, but specific things may reduce its general appeal and number of potential buyers.

These include overly modified cars, colour changes or wraps, cloth seats, higher than average mileages, or those that have been insurance write-offs (Cat C or D) or have a salvage title. Service history is important to most buyers, so examples that are overdue an inspection service or have gaps in their history, and self-serviced cars with no receipts or proof of work carried out are likely to cause the average buyer concern, or a reason to expect a reduced price. A cherished Z4 can cover 200,000 miles without major drama, so don't be too concerned, as long as the price reflects this.

5 Before you view
– be well informed

To avoid a wasted journey, and the disappointment of finding that the car does not match your expectations, it helps if you're clear about the model you want. If you are looking for a car in a hurry, have a think about areas in which you may compromise: for example, colour, or features such as sat nav.

Start checking current values of the model you are interested in by looking at car magazines, websites such as Autotrader, eBay, and Pistonheads, and owners clubs and forums.

Enjoy the engine note with the roof down.

If you would like to try before you buy, think about joining an owners club, Z4 forum or social media group, to see if a local owner is willing to take you out for a drive. This is especially useful if this is your first open top car, or if you are unsure whether you will physically fit into it, or if a particular engine has enough power.

Your first Z4 decision will probably be whether you prefer an E85 Roadster or E86 Coupé, followed by manual or automatic transmissions,

A local owner might take you for a drive. (Credit Peter Gillespie)

and a four- or six-cylinder engine, before getting down to colour preferences and specifications.

Think about what questions you want to ask before you pick up the telephone. Some of these points might appear basic, but when you're excited about the prospect of buying your dream modern classic, it's amazing how some obvious things slip the mind.

Roadster or Coupé?
You may already know your preference, in which case skip to the next paragraph. Alternatively, there is no substitute for trying both. The Coupé has a larger boot, a sleek 'double bubble' roof line, and is perhaps slightly quieter and more secure, but was made from 2006 only, and with only the larger engines. The Roadster is far more widespread, is slightly cheaper, and allows you to feel the sun and hear the engine more clearly with the roof down. It is fractionally lighter than the Coupé, and has a wider choice of engine.

Manual or automatic?
Most drivers will know whether they want a manual or automatic gearbox, although

for some, the lines are slightly blurred. There are two types of automatic gearbox to choose from: Steptronic is a more conventional torque-converting auto, and SSG (otherwise known as SMG) is a semi automatic 'box which is essentially a six-speed manual gearbox and clutch, but with clever actuators that select the gear for you, and no clutch pedal. The SMG gearbox allows the engine to rev, and sounds like a manual, with similar performance and fuel economy. The trade-offs are the gear change is slower than a manual, it's not as smooth as a full automatic, and isn't happy holding on a hill without using the brake (it will roll backwards, or you risk burning the clutch).

Some automatics (of both types) were fitted with paddle shift levers behind the steering wheel, whilst some owners have retrofitted them.

Multi-function wheel.

The manual gearboxes are usually five-speed in the smaller engined cars (up to 2.5-litre) and six-speed in the rest. However, after 2006 all face-lift manual cars became six-speed. All have well-judged gear ratios, with a reassuringly firm feel to the clutch pedal and gear change motion, although the shift is not as slick as in the Honda S2000 or Mazda MX5, for example. It is at least positive, and you are never in doubt that you have selected a gear. It is worth noting that the 3.4-litre Alpina Roadster S and 3.2-litre M models were available in manual transmission only.

Engine

All engines fitted to the Z4 are brisk enough to keep up in traffic, so it's just a question of how much power you want. Specifications changed throughout the life of the cars, particularly in 2006 during the face-lift. All except the 2-litre engine are six-cylinder, and are smooth and sound sporty. The 2-litre, four-cylinder engine that became available in 2005 is well liked by owners, with lower emissions and good fuel economy, but does have some documented issues (see chapter 8) and isn't as pleasing to the ear as the six-cylinders.

The 3-litre engine size was the best selling, available in three different configurations, one of which was US only. The European market had the M54 engine producing 230bhp until 2006, when worldwide models received the Si N52 engine producing 261bhp.

'BMW Individual' customised leather option.

Colour

Owners specifying their new Z4 followed the fashion of the time by choosing muted, neutral colours, so silvers, greys, black and dark blue are the most common shades. Brighter colours were available, they just weren't often chosen, with light colours understandably popular in hotter climates to reflect heat. 'BMW Individual' offered owners the chance to select more unusual colour combinations inside and out for paint, trim and leather. Silvers, greys, red and light blue are good colours for not showing dirt and light scratches. Try to be as open minded as possible about colour, and if the opinion of others is important, look for photos online in the same colour.

Specification

Here is where things get harder. You could probably fill half this book or more by listing what equipment came with which model and in which year, there are just so many combinations! The main areas are:

Seats

Leather, electric, heated M Sports seats are most desirable, followed by regular leather, then cloth. Heated leather seats are very useful in some climates, in Roadsters especially. Electric memory settings give you three driver seat positions, so at a touch of a button the seat returns to the preset position.

Lights

Xenon lights are brightest, and were optional on most models. They came as part of the Lux pack on Alpina S, and were standard on M variants.

Satellite Navigation

Available in a basic 'Business' system with monochrome display in the radio console, or the more commonly seen and far superior 'Professional' flip up, dash-top colour screen. The Professional sat nav is a DVD based

Professional satellite navigation – it looks dated, but it works.

system, with the player located between the backs of the seats in the drop-down compartment. It is a reliable system, and allows you to view the phone's address book (with optional Bluetooth) as well as radio and stations, CD track, and even altitude. By today's standards the screen is low resolution and is showing its age. Thanks to the availability of updated firmware and latest map discs, it is still a functioning system.

Stereo

Three main choices: standard, HiFi and DSP/Carver/Professional/Logic 7 (it is known by a number of names). The standard stereo gives you four or six speakers and is adequate even at speed with the roof down. The HiFi system has ten speakers, including behind the seats, with grilles taking the place of the basic system's storage cubby holes. The Dolby Pro Logic 7 system is both louder, and in theory clearer, however, owners report that setting it up to suit the type of music you listen to can be quite complicated.

Standard Business stereo system has pockets behind the seats.

HiFi, or Professional stereo, has speakers behind the seats.

Extended leather on roof surround.

All units will play MP3 CDs, and models from 2007 onward come with a 3.5mm aux jack for an MP3 player.

PDC
Rear parking sensors. Useful if you regularly need to park the car in tight places, although with a long nose it would have been useful had front sensors been available.

Extended leather
A rare option that adds leather to the inside of the doors (top to bottom), complete windscreen surround, transmission tunnel, and, on the Roadster, the roll hoops. There are many adverts listing extended leather, but rarely do the cars actually have this; leather on the middle of the door cards only comes standard.

Wheels
Wheels are easily changed, so should you find a car that is ideal in all respects except for the style of wheel, you can choose from a healthy second hand market for your preferred alloys. Aftermarket alloys can vary in quality, and be aware that tyres for the popular 19in M3 CSL style wheels don't come cheap. If the rims are kerbed or show sign of corrosion they can be refurbished, providing they are not heavily split or buckled.

Modifications
Cars that have been altered from their standard specification needn't be avoided, providing the modifications are to your taste. For example, you may be thinking ahead about adding a certain style of wheel, lowering the car, or perhaps adding a sporty exhaust? Just check the quality of the parts and their fitting. Modified cars are usually not worth more than a standard example, and in many cases potentially less, and will have a smaller number of potential buyers.

Matching data/legal ownership
Do VIN/chassis, engine numbers and licence plate match the official registration document? Is the owner's name and address recorded in the official registration documents?

For those countries that require an annual test of roadworthiness, does the car have a document showing it complies (an MoT certificate in the UK, which can be verified online at www.gov.uk/check-mot-status or by calling 0845 600 5977)?

If a smog/emissions certificate is mandatory, does the car have one?

If required, does the car carry a current road fund licence/licence plate tag?

Does the vendor own the car outright? Money might be owed to a finance company or bank: the car could even be stolen. Several organisations will supply the data on ownership, based on the car's licence plate number, for a fee. Such companies can often also tell you whether the car has been 'written off' or has a salvage title. Sometimes sellers list a written-off car as a Cat C/D, or on 'VCar.'

A Category C or D car represents an uneconomic insurance write off. These can be a cost effective way of buying a car, but they are harder to sell on, and you need to check the quality of repairs very carefully. In the UK these organisations can supply vehicle data:

HPI – 01722 422 422
AA – 0870 600 0836
DVLA – 0870 240 0010
RAC – 0870 533 3660
Other countries will have similar organisations.

Where is the car?

Is it going to be worth travelling to the next county/state, or even across a border? A locally advertised car, although it may not be exactly what you are looking for, can add to your knowledge for very little effort, so make a visit – it might even be better condition than expected. A Z4 can be an expensive purchase and one you may live with for years, so it is worth putting in the effort to get the right car.

It is always preferable to view at the vendors home or business premises. In the case of a private sale, the car's documentation should tally with the vendor's name and address. Poor light or wet conditions can disguise a multitude of sins, so try to view in daylight on a dry day.

Dealer or private sale

Establish early on whether the car is being sold by its owner or by a trader. A private owner should know the history of the car in their care, including who they bought it from. A dealer may have a more limited knowledge of a car's history, but should have some documentation. They may offer a warranty/guarantee (ask for a printed copy) and finance, but look at the

Try to view on a dry, bright day.

interest rate closely as it is often possible to get a loan from the bank at a cheaper rate.

Typical queries to ask a seller include:

How long have you owned the car or had the car for sale?

Ask for an honest appraisal of the car's condition.

How many previous owners?

What service history do you have (receipts, stamps in service book)?

When was it last serviced?

Confirming some of the important points raised in the advert, as sometimes mistakes are made.

Ask for an honest appraisal of the car's condition. Ask specifically about some of the check items described in chapter 7.

What price would you accept for the car? Don't ask "Would you accept a discount?" as this is too easy for them to refuse. Be prepared to make a lower offer.

That last question is the hardest one to ask, but it can make life much simpler if you can establish a discount before taking up valuable time.

Cost of collection and delivery

A dealer may well be used to quoting for delivery by car transporter. A private owner may agree to meet you halfway, but only agree to this after you have seen the car at the vendor's address to validate the documents.

Dealer or private sale?

Insurance

Check with your existing insurer before setting out, your current policy might not cover you to drive the car if you do purchase it.

How you can pay

Many buyers and sellers are comfortable with an internet bank transfer. A cheque/check will take several days to clear, and the seller may prefer to sell to a cash buyer. A banker's draft (a cheque issued by a bank) is safer than cash, although rarely used these days.

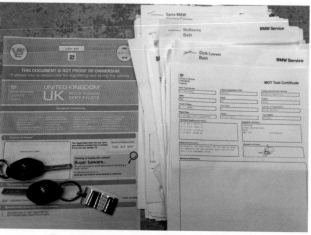

Does the car come with a service history?

Buying at auction?
If the intention is to buy at auction see chapter 10 for further advice.

Professional vehicle check (mechanical examination)
There are often marque/model specialists who will undertake professional examination of a vehicle on your behalf. Owners' clubs will be able to put you in touch with such specialists.

Other organisations that will carry out a general professional check in the UK are –

AA – 0800 085 3007 (motoring organisation with vehicle inspectors)
ABS – 0800 358 5855 (specialist vehicle inspection company)
RAC – 0870 533 3660 (motoring organisation with vehicle inspectors)
Other countries will have similar organisations.

Cracked aftermarket brake disc after heavy track use.

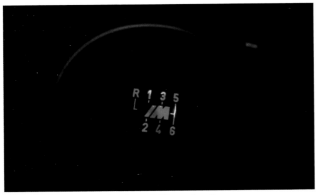

Illuminated M gearknob.

6 Inspection equipment

– these items will really help

This book
Reading glasses (if you need them for close work)
Magnet (not powerful, a fridge magnet is ideal)
Torch (Flashlight)
Overalls and thin rubber gloves (nitrile are ideal)
A mat or rug to crawl on
Mirror on a stick
Digital camera
A clean rag (for checking the oil)
A clean drying towel
OBD2 code reader (optional)
A friend, preferably a knowledgeable enthusiast
A pen to make notes and score, see chapter 9

Before you rush out of the door, gather together a few items that will help as you work your way around the car. This book is designed to be your guide at every step, so take it along and use the check boxes to help you assess each area of the car.

A magnet will help you check if the car is full of filler, but remember that the bonnet is aluminium and the bumpers and side skirts are plastic, so the magnet won't stick to these. Use the magnet to sample the doors, bootlid and front and rear wings, but be careful not to damage the paintwork.

OBD2 code reader.

A torch with fresh batteries will be useful for peering into the wheelarches and under the car.

If you are going to get really involved in your inspection be prepared to get dirty. Take along a pair of overalls and thin rubber gloves. Fixing a mirror at an angle on the end of a stick may seem odd, but you'll probably need it to peer at the underside, sills and crevices of the car.

If you have the use of a digital camera or phone camera take it along so that later you can study some areas of the car more closely. Take a picture of any part of the car that causes you concern, and seek a friend's opinion. Photos will also capture a nice memory of what it looked like should you decide to buy.
A video clip can be taken to record the sound of the engine and exhaust.
Ideally, have a friend or knowledgeable enthusiast accompany you: a second opinion is always valuable.

7 Fifteen minute evaluation
– walk away or stay?

Most Z4 models were made in good numbers so you should have lots to choose from providing you are happy to travel. Models such as the Alpina Roadster S, or M Roadster or Coupé were produced in smaller numbers, therefore occasionally making it a seller's market.

You will by now have asked the right questions of the seller by phone, social media or email, and are feeling reasonably confident that this could be 'the one,' providing the car is as described.

So, you have arrived at the seller's premises and are now looking at what is hopefully a nice, shiny BMW? Your time is precious, as is that of the current owner, so spend 15 minutes looking at the car and asking questions before you decide whether to invest more time with the seller, or agree to politely move on to the next car on your list.

Alpina and M models were made in small numbers.

The owner

Remember it is the car you are buying, not the seller: the appearance of the surroundings or your personal opinion of the seller, whilst a factor, is not proof of a good or bad car.

As these are sports cars that can be used on a regular basis you could be viewing a low or high mileage vehicle, and both could have their drawbacks. A car that is only used for short journeys and garaged for six months of the year may have a different set of issues than one used in all weathers and pounded up and down motorways. You will never know for sure how this or a previous owner has treated the car, so you will have to learn as much as you can from what your eyes and ears tell you and what the paperwork and service history lead you to believe.

Two-seater sports cars are for some an impulse buy, a fashion statement or a box to be ticked. As such, it's common for owners to only keep them for a year or two before moving on. Multiple previous owners needn't be a bad thing, providing they have all kept up the appropriate mechanical care.

Certification

Check that the paperwork, keys and locking wheel nut key are present; don't leave this to the end. Check the

VIN location number one.

chassis number (VIN) on the registration document matches those at the base of the windscreen and in the engine bay on the suspension turret (it is normal for it to be covered by what looks like clear tape).

VIN location number two.

Body condition

Z4s have excellent rust proofing, so you shouldn't see any rusty paintwork, except on high mileage cars. Bend down and look along the flanks of the car on the driver's side, looking in the reflections for ripples or dents; repeat on the passenger side. Z4s have curves and angles everywhere, but they are symmetrical, so you can compare one side of the car to the other if you are unsure whether a particular crease or bulge should be there! Check each panel and door in turn; is the colour even on each panel? Are the gaps between each panel even? Larger gaps each side indicate that either the panels have been removed and then re-attached without sufficient care, or the car has had an accident.

The bumpers and sill covers are plastic and alignment is mostly achieved using plastic clips, so the gaps can made more even if you find they are not perfect.

In terms of light damage from daily driving, the most vulnerable part of a Z4 is the long and low front end.

Crouch down in front of the car and check for stone chips; BMW paint is tough, so excessive chips could indicate a life on the track or the motorway. Use your hand to feel under the front of the bumper for excessive scraping. Look for fine cracking in the paint on the lower part of the front bumper, which occurs when the front end is compressed on kerbs or speed humps. If the weather is wet, use your soft drying cloth to gently wipe away any drops of water to check specific areas of paintwork for scratches, but be very careful and get the permission of the seller – you don't want to scratch the paint if your cloth picks up grit!

Are the fog lights (if fitted) cracked or steamed up? Look through the front upper and lower grilles for stone damaged a/c, oil cooler (M only) or radiator fins, or signs of coolant leaking (coloured water stains).

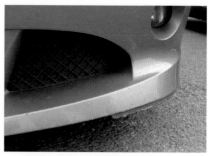

Stone chips are indicative of high mileage.

Panel damage.

If you are looking at a Roadster, carefully check the fabric hood for frayed fabric or excessive chafing. Shiny areas of fabric are to be expected, and occur when the fabric rubs against itself as it is raised and lowered.

Paintwork
BMW paint is strong and durable, but, unusually, has a slight 'orange peel' effect when you look closely in reflections. This is normal, providing that the car has the same finish all over. On the underside of panels, most noticeably on the bonnet, it is normal for the paint to be thinner and also less shiny, having a satin finish where the glossy lacquer is not applied from the factory.

Wheels and tyres
As you travel around the car look at each wheel and tyre in turn. Are the alloy wheels corroded or kerbed? If so allow a cost of around ●60 per wheel for refurbishment or repair.

Corrosion on style 104 wheels.

Are locking wheel nuts fitted (one on each wheel)? If so, ask to see the locking wheel nut key, and check that it fits.

Are tyres matching and of a quality brand? Look, or – even better – feel for even tread wear. Mismatched, cheap tyres may be an indication that an owner or garage is prepared to skimp in other areas. Uneven tread wear could be down to a number of factors, such as poorly maintained tyre pressures, poor alignment (also known as tracking), worn suspension bushes (only likely above 60,000 miles), track driving, or possible accident damage. 'Sawtooth' tread with high and low blocks can produce a droning sound similar to a worn wheel bearing, and new tyres and alignment usually cure this. The outer side walls are prone to damage if run along a kerb during parking, so are there splits, gouges or chunks missing? Each tyre could cost between ●70 and ●150 depending on the size and make of the tyre. Rears tyres are wider, and therefore more expensive than the fronts.

Boot
Start by pressing the unlock button on the key: you should hear the doors unlock. If the remote central locking doesn't work on either key (there should be two), you may have a problem. It is unlikely to be something as simple as a key battery, as Z4s cleverly charge this each time the key is in the ignition.

Open the boot (trunk): on a Roadster this can be done by pressing the button in the driver's footwell by the door aperture (note: this is also where the bonnet/hood release lever is located), and on the Coupé by pressing the BMW

Coupé boot access.

badge on the bootlid. On both models, pressing and holding the button on the key furthest from the blade unlocks the boot, allowing you to lift it up.

Hydraulic rams on each side should be strong enough to hold the lid up in its highest position. If you are looking at a Coupé, the larger, heavier bootlid could start to lower if the hydraulic rams get old and lose pressure, but these are easily replaced.

Z4s come with two identical keys.

The underside of a Coupé bootlid is one of the only areas where you may see a small sign of rust. Water runs down the rear window and collects in a small puddle at the base of the window and bootlid, nicknamed the 'bird bath,' leading to a small rust patch on the underside. Whilst this is unsightly, it is unlikely to cause any other issues, but to date BMW has been very good at honouring their 12-year anti-corrosion warranty providing they believe the bodywork inspection has taken place regularly.

The battery is housed under the boot floor except on M models, where it is in the right-hand corner inside a box. M models have a mobility kit consisting of a bottle of tyre sealant and

Water collects at the base of the Coupé window.

a compressor; check these are present. Ideally the sealant should be within its use by date. A small black vinyl pouch houses very basic tools and the screw-in towing eye.

On the Coupé, open and close the fabric luggage cover; it retracts like a roller blind.

Cracked Roadster brake light.

Close the boot and look at the centre brakelight, housed here. Is it cracked? This is fairly common on the Roadster, caused by poor design and possibly over-tightening during fitting. It is a cosmetic issue rather than one likely to cause a problem.

Under the bonnet/hood

Pull the release handle in the driver's footwell. Slightly lift the bonnet and feel for the release catch just to the right of centre – lift this, and gently raise the bonnet. Hydraulic rams help to lift it and keep it fully raised. If the bonnet tries to close under the force of gravity, budget for replacement struts. They are not expensive, and take just minutes to change.

The engine bay is huge and makes access for inspection and maintenance easy by modern standards. You can actually see and admire the engine itself, without an excess of plastic covers.

The engine bay should be cool ideally, so you get the chance to start the car from cold. All engines, except the 2-litre N52, have a red-handled dipstick on the right side of the engine as you face the car from the front.

Use the clean rag you have brought along to check the oil colour. If the seller claims it has just been serviced, the oil should be a clear or slightly golden colour. If

it is black it has not just been changed! N52 cars have sensors for both oil level and condition displayed on the dash.

Take off the oil filler cap on the top of the engine cover; inspect the underside for white emulsion that looks a little like mayonnaise. Cars in colder climates that are used occasionally only are more likely to have signs of this. It could indicate a head gasket failure, where coolant mixes with the engine oil, but this is rare on a Z4.

Check the paintwork around the perimeter of the engine bay, looking for repairs or mismatched paintwork. It is normal for the paint to appear matt compared to the exterior paint, but should be even in finish and colour.

Alpina 3.4-litre engine – note the red dipstick.

Serious fluid leaks are uncommon, but spend a minute shining your torch in every nook and cranny to check for oil or coolant leaks. Oil leaks from the top of the engine usually indicate an old or cracked cam cover seal, which is not too difficult or expensive to replace. Check the coolant expansion tank on the right of the radiator for leaks, with tell-tale signs of dried, coloured coolant. Leave the bonnet open for the tests that follow.

Interior

Open both doors in turn. The window glass should drop by a small amount, which provides clearance so the glass doesn't catch the roof. If it doesn't, the window regulator requires replacement. Check wear to the driver's seat bolster and base: it can reflect the mileage of the car. Low mileage cars with excessive wear should ring alarm bells, as although it is reputedly difficult to 'clock' a Z4, it isn't impossible, with companies in the past advertising 'mileage correction' services. If necessary, adjust the seat and get in.

Check for seat wear.

The interior layout is refreshingly simple – almost basic, having been designed with a certain retro simplicity. Making certain the car is not in gear or drive, and that the parking brake is on, turn the key two clicks, checking that the various warning lights come on. Is the mileage as advertised? How many miles are left before the next service? Start the car without pressing the throttle (doing so on a modern car could damage the catalytic convertors).

The car should start easily after cranking for just a second or two, and the dash warning lights should go out. As the bonnet is still open the engine will be a little louder than you expect, but there shouldn't be any nasty rattles or knocks when starting. For the first minute of running, a secondary air pump may whir away in the engine bay. If the air temperature is cold, expect to see steam from the exhaust(s), which should clear once the engine is hot.

If it is a manual car, depress the clutch. Does it feel very heavy, or can you feel a pulsing? If so, it could indicate a replacement is due soon, although clutches often last beyond 100k miles. When the clutch is depressed the engine note may change slightly, which is normal. With the clutch depressed fully, try to engage all gears – this should be possible without any kind of crunching, or the feeling that the car wants to drive off! In an automatic car, place your foot on the brake then slide

Steam is normal in cold weather.

the lever to D (drive). The engine note may change slightly, and you might feel a slight clunk, but nothing more. Do the same to reverse, and then return to neutral or park.

Turn on the interior fan to minimum and press the A/C button, represented by a snowflake. Again, the engine note should change as the compressor starts working; a rattle or grumble at the same time could be a tensioner or A/C pump bearing.

Any squealing or grumbling noises coming from the engine bay could be belts, tensioner pulleys, water pump, or, if the note changes when turning on the lights, possibly the alternator.

With the engine still running get out of the car and walk to the rear, checking the exhaust for blue smoke, and then

Knocking from the S54 engine is not a good sign!

move around to the engine bay with your torch at the ready. If there is any kind of excessive fluid leak (other than dripping water from the A/C), rattle or knocking from the engine bay or blue smoke from the exhaust, I would suggest walking away and finding another car.

Close the bonnet and return to the inside of the car. Turn off the air-conditioning and adjust the temperature to suit.

Operate the windscreen wipers. If you hear a mechanical squeak it may be possible to cure by lubricating the wiper linkages. The linkages can fail and pop off, but can sometimes be repaired, either using repair clips from eBay at a cost of ●5, or by drilling a hole and using a thin screw, washer and nyloc nut. Worst case scenario, a brand new replacement linkage assembly is around ●450 from BMW, or less for a pattern part.

Electric roof fully lowered, showing invaluable wind deflector.

Blocked rubber drain grommet.

If you're looking at a Roadster, it is now time to lower the roof. In most models this requires just a simple press of a button low down below the heater controls, in front of the gearlever. Press and hold the button and you will hear the hydraulic motor whirr. The windows lower half way, and the roof quickly retracts in about ten seconds from start to finish. Keep your finger on the button until the red light stops flashing – if you keep your finger pressed for just a little longer, the windows will close. Hesitation or unwillingness for the roof to retract should be a cause for concern.

In a base model this is a manual operation, using a single handle above the interior mirror. Turning this pushes the hood back behind you.

The roof motor is a weakness of the Z4, as the motor floods if roof drains are not cleared. Ask the seller about the roof drains – if they don't know what you are talking about, assume these have not been cleared. Should you go on to buy the car, I would recommend you have them cleared at the earliest opportunity – more on this later.

Now raise the roof. The automatic closure should be a smooth action, and as the roof closes above your head it may clang slightly against the top of the windscreen surround. This is normal, as long as it doesn't seem too violent. Keep your finger pressed on the button until the red light goes out.

8 Key points
– where to look for problems

If, at this point, you feel this is not the right car for you, be polite and walk away. If things are looking good, however, the following is a list of some of the problems you could find, but don't let this list put you off. Z4s are generally very reliable cars, and ticking off the points on this list should help you establish whether or not the car you are considering is a good one.

If you have brought along an inexpensive OBD2 code reader, now is the time to plug it in, reading any stored error codes with the engine or ignition on.

The ABS pump and its control unit have been known to fail, although this is fairly unusual; dash warning lights combined with the relevant error code can diagnose this problem. An ABS pump from BMW is in excess of ●2200, although specialists can repair them for a fraction of the cost.

Read error codes with a handheld reader.

If the car is parked on a flat surface, check the gaps between the top of the tyre and the wheelarches. If the gaps on adjacent sides don't match and the car looks lopsided, this could indicate a broken spring: a common BMW problem, which partly explains why fitting thicker lowering springs is popular.

Whilst looking at the wheels, shine your torch through the spokes at the discs. Light surface rust can occur in hours, especially after washing a car, and is nothing to be concerned about. Heavy rust deposits on the braking surface, or a pronounced lip that you can feel with your finger on the outer edge of the braking surface, could indicate that disc replacements may be required. If you take the car for a test drive, check to see if the rust disappears afterwards.

Broken rear springs are common.

The Roadster's roof motor is located behind the left seat (as viewed from behind the car), out of sight below the roof. If you are viewing a Roadster in a quiet area, walk to the left side of the car and position your ear above the rear wing, near the base of the roof. Ask someone to rock the car from side to side, and listen for water sloshing. If necessary, try this again with the roof down. If you can hear water it is an indication that the roof drains are blocked. Providing the roof motor raises and lowers the hood with ease, it is probably worth the gamble that the roof motor is healthy, and clearing the drains from underneath will prevent the risk of water damage. Worst case scenario, track down a specialist on an owners' forum who can revive the pump and even relocate it to the boot, from ●200.

The electric power steering system can suffer from a 'sticky' feeling at various points in the wheel's travel, particularly straight ahead, and this is more common in pre-face-lift models, for which the tolerance setting for the mesh between the electric motor and the column was too tight – on a hot day the plastic on the gears expands, causing a notchy feel to the steering, which disappears when the car cools. This may also be due to a lack of lubrication in the universal joints at the bottom end of the steering column (accessible from the engine bay).

There are a couple of common fixes. One is to adjust the ring that controls the electric motor/column, the other is to fit a grease nipple in the column housing. If you are very unlucky, a replacement rack is needed at ●2700 from BMW, plus steering angle sensor reset – or fit a refurbished unit, maybe even a hydraulic E46 setup.

In section 7 you started the engine. If blue smoke was noted, this indicated oil burning, which we examine in chapter 9 during the test drive. The M54 engine fitted to the 2.2-, 2.5- and 3-litre pre-face-lift Roadster is occasionally known for oil burning. This could be due to the CCV (Crankcase Ventilation) hoses or valve splitting (more common in colder climates), and/or piston oil control rings sticking. The CCV allows oil vapours to return to the sump, but it can malfunction and draw oil directly into the air intake, before being burnt. This burnt oil can coke up the oil control rings allowing recirculating oil to enter the cylinders. The CCV is available from BMW as a cold weather version where the hoses have foam insulation, this may help cure the problem.

Crankcase valve CCV.

A product called Seafoam can be pured down the sparkplug holes and left to soak. This dissolves the carbon on the piston oil control rings, allowing them to seal again. The CCV can even be removed and replaced with a PCV valve that increases vacuum to help the oil control rings seal, together with an oil catch can filled with media to prevent the oil vapour being sucked into the inlet and burned.

The face-lift 2-litre N46 and the 2.5- and 3-litre N52 engines have a known issue with their electric water pump, which can fail, overheating the car and leaving it in limp home mode, sadly with little warning. Preventative maintenance is the best cure.

The 2-litre N46 timing chain tensioners (plastic) can weaken or fail, giving rise to a slapping or excessive ticking noise, most noticeable from a cold start. Sometimes an engine warning light is thrown, but not always. This tensioner fault increases wear on the sprockets and chain, eventually leading to replacement. While the parts are cheap, the labour is high, with quotes around ●1000 not uncommon. It is best to replace the tensioner for the improved later type by 100,000 miles, before failure occurs.

Rubber intake air hoses can split, throwing up engine warning codes that relate to excessive unmetered air. This can cause the engine to run poorly. It is almost impossible to find a hose split until you start removing a few items from the engine bay – not something you will want to do when viewing a car. It is the code itself that gives you the clue. Clearing the code should immediately improve the running of the car until it returns.

Bleeding anti-dazzle mirror.

Cars equipped with anti-dazzle rear and optional side mirrors can 'bleed' their fluid, leaving bubbles or a yellowish tide mark behind the glass. At this point the anti dazzle function will not work. Replacement units from BMW are expensive, but there are companies who can repair them for half the price. Some owners fix these themselves with help from online guides.

9 Serious evaluation
– 60 minutes for years of enjoyment

Score each section using the boxes as follows: 4 = excellent; 3 = good; 2 = average; 1 = poor. The totting up procedure is detailed at the end of the chapter. Be realistic in your marking!

Sports cars are often bought with the heart rather than the head. However, the Z4 is a car that can be viewed as a sensible purchase. You may have now decided to buy the car, and are double-checking for any deal-breakers.

Body

④ ③ ② ①

Whilst the Z4 has excellent corrosion resistance don't let this make you complacent. Look carefully around wheelarches, where salt and mud can accumulate. Any bubbling through the paint will be more serious on the inside. The scuttle cover by the boot can very occasionally see slight rust, and when opening the boot, doors and bonnet check that any accumulations of leaves or dirt are not hiding rust (put your gloves on and have a grub around). Very slight surface rust to the slam panel and bolt heads at the front of the car is normal in wetter climates.

Z4 has excellent corrosion resistance.

Security

④ ③ ② ①

Standard fit security is good, with alarm, immobiliser and locking wheel nuts. It is unusual to find an aftermarket system fitted to a Z4. A tracker is occasionally found and worthwhile, however, most require some sort of fee to transfer into your ownership, as well as an ongoing subscription.

Wheels

④ ③ ② ①

It is almost a given that wheels will have signs of wear, whether through kerbing, lacquer damage, or, more unusually, splitting or buckling. Cost for

Check wheels carefully – these 135M alloys look fine.

refurbishment will vary, but to ensure an even colour match it makes sense to get all four wheels done at the same time, ideally coinciding with replacing worn tyres. Cost for removing tyres, light damage repair, powder coating and refitting is typically costs around ●300 for a set of four.

Owners sometimes fit spacers to move the wheels closer to the outside of the car's bodywork, to improve the appearance by filling the wheelarches. The safest

Damaged wheel and tyre.

Headlight washers can be fitted to Halogen as well as Xenon lights.

way of achieving this is using hubcentric types of spacer. Ask the seller if they know what type were fitted, and if longer bolts are used.

Left-hand drive

With good availability of right- and left-hand drive cars, there are no known conversions of the steering wheel side. Those travelling from the UK to Europe will be pleased to know that it is easy to adjust the beam pattern, whether the car has Halogen or Xenon bulbs. Access to the rear of the light units is gained by removing the plastic panel in the black wheelarch (a large coin is ideal), then moving a small lever up or down as required to alter the left beam cut-off; this is usually done by feel, and can be fiddly the first time. Make sure the headlights are switched off when making this adjustment: Xenons are very high voltage.

Rear underside

The Z4 is low, so checking underneath may prove difficult without a ramp or jack and stands. The Z4 has two sill jacking points on each side, plus a central, round jacking point located behind the engine. The exhaust is the first item to check. It is stainless steel as standard, therefore should be relatively rust free, so focus on the joints and flanges between each section. If an aftermarket system has been fitted, check the fitting and look for evidence of exhaust gases leaking through joints, with tell-tale black soot marks. Buying clamps from BMW, plus the time taken to fit over the flanges, can be costly. Thankfully, much cheaper and easier to fit aftermarket two-piece stainless steel replacements are available.

Exhaust rubbers are strong, but over time can go weak and perish. If the tail pipes don't line up perfectly in the aperture of the rear bumper, and the exhaust appears undamaged, some adjustment is possible on the exhaust mounts and by loosening the back box bolts.

Next look at the CV boots – these rubber bellows will split in time, and fling black grease out of the joint onto the surrounding chassis parts, making a split more obvious. Gently squeeze the rubber boots whilst looking for cracks; a split boot will eventually mean damage to the CV joint if left unattended, an expensive part to replace.

There are two alloy strips that run diagonally from the chassis towards the diff. Garages have occasionally been known to jack up the car from these and bend them! Differential seals have been known to leak on the M models; a specialist will charge around ●300 to change input and driveshaft seals.

In front of the rear wheels and slightly hidden away by the rear trailing arm bush is where the roof drains exit on each side. Strainers are fitted on the bottom to prevent debris from entering the drain. These get blocked with leaves, so check them.

Follow the brake lines from the back of the car to each rear brake calliper. Although they are plastic coated, the lines can still corrode.

Front underside

Again, some of this section assumes you have access to the underside by safely

Old radiators can sag, and eventually leak.

using a jack and stands or a lift. Much of the engine bay is hidden from view by an undertray, aiding aerodynamics and reducing the risk of dirt entering and damaging the engine bay. Helpfully, BMW placed a small cover beneath the sump plug to make oil changes simple. Remove the cover and check for leaks from the sump plug. Is the allen key plug damaged through over-tightening?

Look carefully for signs of any fluid leaks, namely oil or coolant, which will have been blown backwards towards the rear of the car, leaving an oily residue. Radiators can sag at the bottom with age, eventually splitting. M models have hydraulic power steering, leaks are rare.

Whilst damage caused by rocks or speed humps striking the underside could happen, it is usually the front bumper or undertray that takes the brunt rather than items further back.

Sill covers are plastic, so if scraped can be replaced.

If you have sufficient clearance to get under the car and can use a pry bar, you could gently check for play in suspension bushings or anti-roll bar bushes. If not, then the test drive may highlight any play through knocking or banging.

Check the brake fluid lines are corrosion free. The back side of the brake disc surface should either be shiny metal or have a light coasting of rust, with no pronounced lip. Ignore rust around the edges of the disc, this is normal. You may just be able to see the thickness of the brake material left, although this is usually a 'wheels off' job, and pads are not too expensive to replace.

Broken undertray and bumper plastics.

M models made before March 2008 have been known to break or even lose their engine mount bolts on the left (exhaust) side of the engine, allowing the engines to sit low enough to bang on the anti-roll bar. Stronger grade steel replacements are available; just check they are present and tight.

Cockpit 4 3 2 1

Take a second look at the cockpit area, which should now be more familiar to you. Are there any signs of ill-treatment?

The seats could be 'Sensatec' fabric, 'Active Sports' half leather with cloth centre panels, or full leather. Leather came in basic Oregon, New England or top of the range Nappa. The grain, softness and quality of the leather is slightly different between all three. New England seats have a longitudinal recessed inset down the middle of the

Check that the sat nav disc works.

Embroidered
Alpina seats.

main central seat bottom, for Oregon the same piece is solid across to the bolsters. Nappa was standard on the M models. The Alpina Roadster S had embroidered leather seats as standard along with leather on the dash, centre console, door handles, steering wheel spoke and trim.

All seat coverings resist wear well, but check the driver's bolster which is vulnerable to damage, as it gets rubbed by the driver sliding into the seat. Has the seller tried to cover up the wear using a dye or shoe polish? Small scuffs to leather or pulled threads in fabric can often be professionally repaired with astonishing results, but holes in leather or heavy wear may require new panels from a specialist, or even a new seat cover from BMW. The latter is not cheap at around ●1000 – more if they are heated, as the elements are encapsulated between the leather outer and the insulation beneath.

Floor mats were standard on the Z4, and can be replaced for ●100.

The carpet comes in two large pieces, front and rear. Check carefully for rips, burns or holes, as each are over ●500.

Start the car and move the seats in every direction. Turn on the heated seats if present – the first touch should show three lights, and on this maximum heat setting you start to feel warmth within a few minutes. During this time check that every electronic function and button works.

Pull down the panel between the seats. This has small storage areas together with the optional DVD sat nav drive and six-CD multi-changer. If present, check that both function. If the panel that pulls down contains a button that pictures a voice and a slot for an old phone, this car has Bluetooth for wireless phone voice calls. It isn't sophisticated enough to play streaming music, but call quality is acceptable.

M embossed
Nappa leather.

Steering wheel ④ ③ ② ①

All Z4 steering wheels are the same diameter, with the sport types feeling chunky to the touch. The horn is operated by pressing the centre boss. The standard wheel has no buttons, and many have the optional leather

Bluetooth-equipped car with DVD drive
for sat nav.

covering, together with leather gearknob and manual gearbox gaiter. The multi-function wheel adds buttons for controlling the radio, and optional Bluetooth and sat nav with speech control. The M and Alpina models have their respective signature colours in the stitching. The steering wheel coverings have excellent resistance to wear, although the stitching can get grubby, but nothing a gentle clean can't rectify. Royale Steering Wheels in the UK perform an excellent re-covering service should it be necessary, or you fancy a change of design.

Worn thumb grips.

Gloss black dash trim.

Wood trim is a high quality veneer.

The one area of the wheel that is prone to wear is where your thumbs rest at the quarter to three position. The plastic here has a thin rubberised coating that wears off, showing patches of white underneath as the black plastic thins. These thumb rests can be replaced, although the job is fiddly.

The M model gearknob illuminates red when the lights are switched on. If this doesn't work it has either been replaced by the popular, heavier ZHP/M5 knob, or the brittle wires have broken underneath the gaiter. This is easy to repair with new wire and a soldering iron.

Console

The dash and gear surround trim came in a large variety of metals, genuine wood veneers, plastics, black gloss, carbon effect leather (M only) or stitched leather (Alpina only). Thankfully, all can be changed depending on taste or damage.

Glass

Check the windscreen for chips or cracks. The side windows can get scratched as grit or dirt rubs between the glass and the outer weather strip. It is also normal to see faint vertical stripes on the inside of the glass. This is due to a poor design that allows the glass to touch against grease from the electric window mechanism, transferring it to the glass. You can clean it each time, but it will return; thankfully, no damage occurs, it's just annoying cosmetically. Having someone shine a torch from the outside may help you see small chips or scratches you might otherwise not notice.

Unusually, the door mirrors are permanently heated on the Z4 and, over the years, this can soften and weaken the glue that holds the glass in place. Gently wiggle the mirror glass to see if they are loose, as they can fall out at random and smash, potentially damaging the bodywork as they go.

Road test

This is the most important part of the serious evaluation stage, and one you have probably been most looking forward to.

Whether you or the seller will be driving depends on the individual circumstances, and whether you are covered by insurance. If this is a private purchase, I would be happy to be a passenger to begin with. It will give you a chance to look and listen for things you may not be aware of as a driver.

You are not judging the driver on their skills behind the wheel, but their actions may indicate how they have treated the car. Suggest a test route that covers a mixture of roads, but especially the type of roads you expect to be driving.

Orange lights and oil gauge temperature indicates a cold S54 M engine.

Warming up

You should have already started the engine at least once, so the warming up process has begun. The car should always be fully warmed before using full throttle or high revs; not doing so causes premature damage and wear. If the owner proceeds to show you the full performance of the car right away, this could indicate this is their normal driving style and is potentially a cause for concern.

Engine coolant warms far sooner than oil so once the coolant is at normal operating temperature drive for a further 5 minutes before using the full performance of the car; only M models have an oil temperature gauge. M models don't have a coolant gauge, instead they have a series of orange and red lights around the rev counter. These lights represent the coolant temperature and quickly extinguish, leaving the last orange and red light continually lit. You must not use sustained full throttle or high revs on M models until the oil temperature gauge slowly rises to its normal operating temperature above 75 degrees C/165F, this can take anything up to 15 minutes driving to achieve.

The 2-litre engine can develop cracks in its exhaust manifold, most noticeable whilst the engine is cold. In mild cases this could sound like a blowing exhaust, if the split is larger the Z4 can sound like a tractor!

Suspension

It can be tempting when test driving a sports car to become intoxicated and plant your right foot a little too enthusiastically, but the aim is not to see how fast it accelerates, brakes and corners, but to look, listen and feel for potential problems.

Whilst waiting for the car to fully warm up, listen for knocks from the suspension. The ride on all Z4s is firm, so expect to get the odd crash over pot holes. You may even hear the odd rattle from the interior trim as a result, but knocking sounds are not normal.

Changing old rubber bushes will sharpen handling.

If need be, aim for one or two small dips, ridges or drain covers to get the suspension really working. Knocking or thumping could be anti-roll bar links, suspension bushes or top mounts – it's hard to tell which, and it only takes a small amount of play to make a big noise. Cars with more than 75k miles may benefit from replacement suspension bushes, perhaps longer lasting poly bushes, which revitalises handling and feel.

Geometry setup; here, using the string method.

Expensive ABS pump.

Is the car pulling to one side, either when accelerating or braking? Is the steering wheel lined up straight when you are driving straight? Tramlining is more pronounced on cars with large wheels fitted, but could just as easily be an indication that tracking (alignment) is needed or that rubber suspension bushes have become tired. Z4s have a number of geometry adjustments on both the front and rear, that can make a big difference to handling and how willing the car is to turn in, and track straight ahead.

Brakes   [1]

Find a stretch of straight, wide road with no traffic, and, after warning your passenger, brake firmly, but not so hard as to trigger the ABS. The car may pull slightly to one side if the road is cambered, but should reduce speed without drama. Any banging or dramatic veering to either side is a cause for concern. The expensive (●2200) ABS pump can fail, but warning lights on the dash alert you to this. The standard brakes on all models should feel strong and sharp. If they are underwhelming, the brake pads or fluid could be old. If the car has been stored for a while or the

brake surfaces are rusty, then the first few times you brake may be noisy as the rust is ground off. Any wobbling or pulsing through the pedal may be due to warped discs or pad material that has transferred to the disc; this may improve after braking a few times.

Traction   [2] [1]

The traction and stability controls are very effective at countering excessive wheelspin or sliding, but they can't beat physics, of course. Entering a tight corner too fast in the wet may end in tears, so save it for the track! Sometimes the traction control

Enjoy the test drive, but not too much! (Courtesy Elizabeth Smitheram)

is just a little too intrusive, so pressing the DSC/DTC button once allows wheelslip, whilst still leaving the stability control active. A long press and hold turns off all safety systems except the anti-lock brakes, which are always on. A short press of the same button switches the safety systems back on. Some enterprising owners have worked out how to load on the M3 CSL 'M Track' mode onto M models, giving an excellent halfway setting on the stability control.

All Z4 models except the M have open differentials. The M diff is very effective on road and track, and more than capable of lighting up the rear tyres into a power slide or drift. Limited slip diffs for other models are available from companies including OSGiken and Quaife.

Sport button

4️⃣ 3️⃣ 2️⃣ 1️⃣

The first thing to clear up is that this doesn't make the Z4 faster, it just makes it feel that way. By altering the fly-by-wire throttle settings, sport mode gives you full throttle much sooner in the pedal travel. You could of course just press the throttle pedal down further in normal driving mode and get the same performance.

The sport button makes the Z4 feel faster.

In non-M models it reduces the electric power steering assistance, and cruise control accelerates faster. It is with the automatics you notice the sport button most, with each gear revving higher and with a faster gearshift.

Steering

4️⃣ 3️⃣ 2️⃣ 1️⃣

Through a variety of tight and open corners, try to feel what the front wheels are doing. Does the electric power steering feel 'sticky' at various points in the wheel's travel, particularly straight ahead? (If so, see chapter 8.)

The Z4M hydraulic power steering is trouble-free.

Gearchange

4️⃣ 3️⃣ 2️⃣ 1️⃣

The manual is perhaps not the best that BMW has ever produced, and newcomers may find it clunky by modern standards, but it's certainly positive and durable.

Find a hill and at 30mph accelerate hard in third gear, checking for any clutch slip. If you are driving an automatic Z4, you should try it in Drive (D), then at some stage slide the lever across to the + and - symbols, and by pressing forwards and backwards, cycle through each gear. If the car has paddles behind the steering wheel, pull/push on these in the same way, to check you can select each gear.

The semi-automatic (SSG) gearbox can achieve a smoother gear change if you lift your foot off the throttle each time you anticipate a change or select a gear yourself. While you can make full throttle gear changes with the semi-automatic gearbox, doing so will not be smooth. Don't use the throttle to hold this car stationary on a hill, or the clutch can overheat. Instead use the footbrake

Change gear manually using the + and -.

or handbrake until you are ready to move. Face-lift manual cars have hill start assist, where the brakes are held on for a few seconds if the car is in gear and your foot is on the clutch. It is easy to get used to and works well.

An 'inspection two' gearbox oil change often helps with the smoothness of the gears, as does removing the 'CDV,' or clutch delay valve. This is a one-way restrictor valve that BMW fitted to manual Z4s to slow the engagement of the clutch, but most owners report that removing it (from underneath the car) improves the clutch action and gear change.

On a suitable road and with the engine fully warmed up, run the engine to higher speeds through the gears, listening for misfire, clutch slip, hesitation or unwillingness to rev. Z4 engines are equipped with dual VANOS where the camshafts can rotate and alter their timing to deliver improved torque, power and economy, depending on what the driver asks of the car. The VANOS system is dependent on oil pressure, and, over time, the seals can allow some oil to pass by, leading to a loss of torque below 3000rpm. A home mechanic can change these, or a BMW specialist will be familiar with this job. Whilst the VANOS can fail, it is unusual. N52 engines in the face-lift Si models can, on rare occasions, suffer from camshaft bearing cap wear that also reduces VANOS oil pressure.

Replacing Vanos seals on an M54 2.5 engine.

All Z4 engines deliver their maximum power at high revs: above 5800rpm, and up to as high as 7900rpm in the case of the M engines. Don't be afraid to use these revs on the test drive when safe to do so, and with the permission of the owner.

When accelerating hard, look in the mirrors to check for smoke. In the unlikely event you do see smoke and it decreases each time you accelerate, this points to possible CCV failure, which may not be too serious, as mentioned in the previous chapter.

M engines with their solid lifters can sound a bit 'tappety' – this is normal, and you become most aware of it when driving along a row of parked cars or a verge where sound bounces back. An inspection service can help reduce this sound, as the valve clearances are adjusted back into spec. Whilst rare, the S54 3.2 engine can wear its rod-bearing shells if it has been driven hard from cold, or has very high mileage. Preventative bearing shell replacement at a specialist will cost from ●700 if no wear has taken place to the crank. Best practice is to change the oil and filter more regularly than BMW recommends, and always use the correct weight of oil.

Oil filter access makes regular servicing easy.

Evaluation procedure

Evaluation procedure
Add up the total points.
Score: 72 = excellent; 54 = good; 36 = average; 18 = poor. Cars scoring over 50 will be completely usable and will require only maintenance and care to preserve condition. Cars scoring between 18 and 37 will require some serious work (at much the same cost regardless of score). Cars scoring between 38 and 49 will require very careful assessment of the necessary repair/restoration costs in order to arrive at a realistic value.

10 Auctions
– sold! Another way to buy your dream

Auction pros & cons
Pros: Prices will usually be lower than dealers or private sellers, and you might grab a real bargain on the day. Auctioneers have usually established clear title with the seller.
Cons: You have to rely on a sketchy catalogue description of condition and history. The opportunity to inspect is limited, and the biggest drawback is you cannot drive the car. Auction cars are often a little below par, and may require some work. The estimate is often priced unrealistically low, and it's easy to overpay if you get carried away by 'auction fever.'

Catalogue, entry fee and payment details
When you purchase the catalogue of the vehicles in the auction, it often acts as a ticket allowing two people to attend the viewing days and the auction. The catalogue will contain a brief description of the car, guide price, buyer's premium and details of acceptable forms of payment. At the fall of the hammer an immediate deposit is usually required, the balance payable within 24 hours. There are sometimes payment restrictions, so find out the auctions accepted method. No car will be released before all payments are cleared. Don't forget the buyer's premium and any additional local taxes.

Viewing
In some instances it's possible to view on the day, or days before, as well as in the hours prior to the auction. There are auction officials available who are willing to help out by opening engine and luggage compartments and allowing you to inspect the interior. While the officials may show you the paperwork and start the engine for you, jacking up the car or a test drive is out of the question.

Bidding
Before you take part in the auction, decide your maximum bid – and stick to it!
When it's the turn of your car, attract the auctioneer's attention and make an early bid. The auctioneer will then look to you for a reaction every time another bid is made. Usually the bids will be in fixed increments until the bidding slows, at which point smaller increments are often accepted before the hammer falls.
Assuming that you are the successful bidder, the auctioneer will note your card or paddle number, and from that moment on you are responsible for the vehicle.
If the car is unsold, either because it failed to reach the reserve or because there was little interest, it may be possible to negotiate with the owner, via the auctioneers, after the sale is over.

Successful bid
There are two more things to consider: how to get the car home, and insurance.
Insurance for immediate cover can usually be purchased on site, but it may be more cost-effective to make arrangements with your own insurance company in advance, and then call to confirm the full details.

eBay & other online auctions

This could land you a car at a bargain price, though you'd be foolhardy to bid without examining the car first – something most vendors encourage. A useful feature of eBay is that the geographical location of the car is shown, so you can narrow your choices to those within a realistic radius of home. Be prepared to be outbid in the last few moments of the auction. Remember, your bid is binding, but the car should be as described when you come to view it.

Be aware that some cars offered for sale in online auctions are 'ghost' cars. Don't part with any cash without being sure that the vehicle does actually exist and is as described (usually pre-bidding inspection is possible).

Auctioneers

Barrett-Jackson www.barrett-jackson.com; **Bonhams** www.bonhams.com; **British Car Auctions (BCA)** www.bca-europe.com or www.british-car-auctions.co.uk; **Christies** www.christies.com; **Coys** www.coys.co.uk; **eBay** www.ebay.com or www.ebay.co.uk; **H&H** www.handh.co.uk; **RM Sotheby's** www.rmsothebys.com; **Shannons** www.shannons.com.au; **Silver** www.silverauctions.com

Online auctions can be a good place to find a Z4.

11 Paperwork
– correct documentation is essential!

The paper trail
I would expect a good Z4 to come with a large portfolio of paperwork, accumulated and passed on by a succession of proud owners. This documentation represents the real history of the car, and from it can be deduced the level of care the car has received, how much it's been used, which specialists have worked on it, and the dates of major repairs and restorations. All of this information will be priceless to you as the new owner, so be very wary of cars with little paperwork to support their claimed history. Any self-serviced cars should have receipts for the parts used that tie up with claimed service dates.

Registration documents
All countries/states have some form of registration for private vehicles whether it's like the American 'pink slip' title system or the British 'log book' system.

It is essential to check that the registration document is genuine, that it relates to the car in question, and that all the vehicle's details are correctly recorded, including chassis/VIN and engine numbers (if these are shown). If you are buying from the previous owner, his or her name and address will be recorded in the document: this will not be the case if you are buying from a dealer.

In the UK, the current (Euro-aligned) registration document is named 'V5C.' Make sure the title is transferred to you, and that paperwork is filled out by both parties where required. In the UK registration can now be transferred online without posting the V5.

Roadworthiness certificate
Most country/state administrations require that vehicles are regularly tested to prove they are safe to use on the public highway and do not produce excessive emissions. In the UK that test (the 'MoT') is carried out every three years at approved testing stations, for a fee. In the USA the requirement varies, but most states insist on an emissions test every two years as a minimum, while the police are charged with pulling over unsafe-looking vehicles.

Of particular relevance for older cars is that the certificate issued includes the mileage reading recorded at the test date and any work that is advised, giving you a clue as to what is needed in the future. Ask the seller if previous certificates are available, if not you can find and print past MoT details from the Department Of Transport website www.gov.uk/check-mot-history. Without an MoT the vehicle should be trailered to its new home, unless you insist that a valid MoT is part of the deal.

Road licence
The administration of every country/state charges some kind of tax for the use of its road system, with the actual form of the 'road licence' and how it is displayed varying enormously country to country and state to state.

Whatever the form of the 'road licence,' it must relate to the vehicle carrying it and must be present and valid if the car is to be driven on the public highway legally. The value of the license will depend on the length of time it will continue to be valid.

BMW handbook, including service record.

Changed legislation in the UK means that the seller of a car must surrender any existing road fund licence, and it is the responsibility of the new owner to re-tax the vehicle at the time of purchase and before the car can be driven on the road. It's therefore vital to see the Vehicle Registration Certificate (V5C) at the time of purchase, and to have access to the New Keeper Supplement (V5C/2), allowing the buyer to obtain road tax immediately.

If the car is untaxed because it has not been used for a period of time, the owner has to inform the licensing authorities, otherwise the vehicle's date-related registration number will be lost and there will be a painful amount of paperwork to get it re-registered.

HPI/hidden history certificate

Many cars are reputed to have had a hidden past, such as having been written off, stolen/recovered, had a change of registration number, or still having finance owed. If buying privately, you should always check for this; if buying from a dealership, they should have already checked, therefore ask for a photocopy of this certificate for both peace of mind and guarantee. Don't be lulled into a false sense of security by having a car that has been give an 'all clear,' as plenty of accident repairs go unrecorded.

Service history

Occasionally these cars will have been serviced at home by an enthusiastic (and hopefully capable) owner for a good number of years. As the Z4 gets older, this is something that will become more commonplace. Try to obtain as much service history and other paperwork pertaining to the car as you can. Dealer stamps, or specialist garage receipts, may score most points in the value stakes. However, anything helps in the great authenticity game. Items like the original bill of sale, handbook, parts invoices and repair bills add to the story and character of the car. Even a brochure matching the year of the car's manufacture is a useful document, and something that you may search hard to locate in future years. If the seller claims that the car has been restored, expect receipts and other evidence from a specialist restorer.

If the seller says they have carried out regular servicing, ask what work was completed, when, and seek some evidence of it being carried out. Your assessment of the car's overall condition should tell you whether the seller's claims are genuine.

Restoration photographs
If the seller tells you that the car has been restored, expect to be shown a series of photographs taken while the restoration was underway. Pictures taken at various stages, and from various angles, should help you gauge the thoroughness of the work. If you buy the car, ask if you can have copies of all the photographs, as they form an important part of the vehicle's history.

Online investigation
A bit of homework online can sometimes reveal more about the car you are buying. Z4 owners are often enthusiasts who frequent forums and social media groups, so you can sometimes find posts and write-ups from the current or previous owners, even photos and videos, all of which help build a picture of the car and its treatment.

Previous ownership records
Due to the introduction of important new legislation on data protection, it is no longer possible to acquire, from the British DVLA, a list of previous owners of a car you own, or are intending to purchase. This scenario will also apply to dealerships and other specialists, from who you may wish to make contact and acquire information on previous ownership and work carried out.

Light damage is unlikely to be recorded.

12 What's it worth?
– let your head rule your heart

Condition

If you used the marking system in chapter 9 you'll know whether the car is in Excellent (maybe Concours), Good, Average or Poor condition or, perhaps, somewhere in between these categories.

Trade and consumer price guides exist, although they seem more accurate for mainstream cars rather than sports cars, often undervaluing Z4s. Allowing for seasonal variation, prices for E85 and E86 have been fairly stable for some time.

Your research in chapters 4 and 5 will tell you whether the car you are considering is fair value compared to others on the market.

Desirable options/extras

Heated, electric, leather M sports seats are most popular, along with uprated BMW stereo, Xenon lights, extended leather, and for some people, cruise control, Bluetooth and sat nav.

Undesirable features

Certain colour schemes, a manual roof on the base 2-litre model, cloth seats, and the SSG automatic gearbox divide opinion.

Concours condition face-lift 2.5Si.

At ⬤3000 and below you can find high mileage 2003 and 2004 Roadsters and cars that have a negative history, particularly those with smaller engines. Cars requiring restoration, cosmetic improvement or mechanical fault are certainly found at this price point.

From ⬤3000 to ⬤5000 you find an excellent choice of Roadsters in manual and automatic, including some face-lift cars. This price band should see you find a good, useable car with service history and a choice of specification, sold privately and at independent dealers.

⬤5000 to ⬤7000 should buy you a lovely Roadster with good specification and average or below average miles. The top end of this price band will also see a few high mileage Coupés, perhaps those with less than perfect history.

⬤7000 to ⬤9000 has a mix of the best Roadsters and higher mileage Coupés.

⬤9000 to ⬤12,000 buys you very low mileage, high specification face-lift Roadsters and good examples of Coupés. Closer to ⬤12000 gets you low mileage SE and Sport Coupés.

⬤12,000 to ⬤15,000 are where you find the first M Roadsters and Alpina Roadster S with higher miles or negative history and the very best, concours 3-litre Si Coupés.

⬤15,000 to ⬤19,000 will get you a decent choice of tidy M Roadsters and the best Alpina Roadster S, with higher mileage, useable M Coupés at the low end of this price band.

⬤19,000 up gets you excellent, investment mileage M Roadsters and M

Excellent condition pre-face-lift 3-litre.

Coupés. It is currently M Coupés that are generally commanding the highest prices, from premium used car dealerships and German marque specialists. As magazines increasingly tip the M models as future classics, the very best examples with full history and no imperfections can command in excess of ●30,000

Striking a deal
Negotiate on the basis of your condition assessment, mileage, and fault rectification cost. Also take into account the car's specification. Be realistic about the value, but don't be completely intractable: a small compromise on the part of the vendor or buyer will often facilitate a deal at little real cost. This is where it helps to discuss monies before visiting the car.

13. Do you really want to restore?
– it'll take longer and cost more than you think

With so many cars to choose from it is unusual to choose a Z4 to restore, unless the price is very appealing, it is a rare specification, or you just fancy a restoration project.

BMW parts pricing has the capacity to both shock and pleasantly surprise: some parts are reasonable (especially those shared with the E46 3 series), while the cost of Z4 specific parts, fittings and bolts are sometimes shocking.

Owners groups and eBay can often be the best source for used genuine or new pattern parts.

Thankfully, rust is not much of an issue compared to some other makes and models, particularly if you have previously restored older cars, for which seized, rusty components are a huge issue.

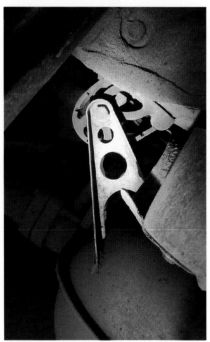

Rubber components can perish over time.

Unless you are very confident with auto electrics it might be best to avoid cars with known loom issues – for example, mouse damage – as all Z4s have Canbus/Multiplex wiring. If the car has been stored for a long time without being charged, or if it has a tired battery, erroneous codes or warning lights can be thrown up. The code reader may help you decipher this.

The first obvious question is why does it need restoration and how long has it been in that condition?

Cars that are halfway through being finished are sometimes worse than those in a completely unrestored state, as you don't have the benefit of dismantling first to know what goes where when you come to rebuild. If the Z4 is already in pieces, you must make sure it is all complete, or, if some parts have already been thrown away due to damage, find out in detail what they are. A dismantled door actually contains hundreds of parts, and if you have to source every screw, clip, panel and more it will take you quite some time and investment.

14 Paint problems
– bad complexion, including dimples, pimples and bubbles

Paint faults generally occur due to lack of protection/maintenance, or poor preparation prior to a respray or touch-up. Some of the following conditions may be present in the car you're looking at.

Orange peel

This appears as an uneven paint surface, similar to the appearance of the skin of an orange, Be aware that BMWs of this era do have a slight amount of orange peel all over, which is a normal feature of the car. Assuming this is a localised fault, it is caused by the failure of atomized paint droplets to flow into each other when they hit the surface. It's sometimes possible to rub out the effect with proprietary paint cutting/rubbing compound or very fine grades of

Very slight orange peel is normal in a Z4.

abrasive paper. A respray may be necessary in severe cases. Consult a bodywork repairer/paint shop for advice.

Cracking

Severe cases are likely to have been caused by too heavy an application of paint (or filler beneath the paint). Also, insufficient stirring of the paint before application can lead to the components being improperly mixed, and cracking can result. Incompatibility with the paint already on the panel can have a similar effect. To rectify the problem it is necessary to rub down to a smooth, sound finish before respraying the problem area. Look for cracking to the bumpers where the car may have slowly had contact during parking, for example. The plastic bumpers can flex and restore their correct shape, but the paint may crack on top. The lower edges of the Z4 front bumper are particularly prone to this.

Crazing

Sometimes the paint takes on a crazed rather than a cracked appearance, when the problems mentioned under 'Cracking' are present. This problem can also be caused by a reaction between the underlying surface and the paint. Paint removal and respraying the problem area is usually the only solution.

Blistering

Almost always caused by corrosion of the metal beneath the paint. Usually perforation is found in the metal, and the

Z4 corrosion is rare. This photo is from an E46 3 Series.

damage is usually worse than that suggested by the area of blistering. The metal has to be repaired before repainting.

Micro blistering
Usually the result of an economy respray, where inadequate heating has allowed moisture to settle on the car before spraying. Consult a paint specialist, but usually damaged paint will have to be removed before partial or full respraying. This can also be caused by car covers that don't 'breathe.'

Fading
Some colours, especially reds, are prone to fading if subjected to strong sunlight for long periods without the benefit of polish protection. Sometimes proprietary paint restorers and/or paint cutting/ rubbing compounds will retrieve the situation. Often a respray is the only real solution. Thankfully BMW paint is good quality, and fading is very rare. The Z4M

Imola Red resists fading well.

exclusive colour, Imola Red, has so far proved excellent at resisting fading, as has Bright Red (Helrot), used on earlier Z4s. The colours on the M badges can fade. You can buy stickers via owners' club forums to neatly replace the coloured section or replace with new badges from BMW, which are applied with adhesive.

Peeling
Often a problem with metallic paintwork when the sealing lacquer becomes damaged and begins to peel off. Poorly applied paint may also peel. The remedy is to strip and start again! This is more likely to be a problem with cars kept outside in hot climates.

Dimples
Dimples in the paintwork or clear coat lacquer are caused by the residue of polish (particularly silicone types) not being removed properly before respraying. Paint removal and repainting is the only solution.

Dents
Small dents are usually easily cured by the 'Dentmaster,' or an equivalent process, that sucks or pushes out the dent (as long as the paint surface is still intact). Companies offering dent removal services usually come to your home or workplace: consult your telephone directory or search online.

The undersides of panels are matt.

15 Problems due to lack of use
– just like their owners, BMW Z4s need exercise

Cars, like humans, are at their most efficient if they exercise regularly. A run of at least ten miles, once a week, is recommended, and is certainly better than just starting a car, idling in the garage.

Seized components
Pistons in callipers, slave and master cylinders can seize.

The clutch may seize if the plate becomes stuck to the flywheel due to corrosion, although this is almost unheard of in a Z4.

Pistons can seize in the engine bores due to corrosion.

Certain compounds of brake pad with metallic content rust to a brake disc in a matter of days if they stay wet after washing, let alone long-term storage. The handbrake shoes operate inside the centre of the rear discs, like a drum brake would. It is rare that they seize, but it is possible in damp conditions if the handbrake has been left on. If the brakes are seized, they are usually freed by starting the car and attempting to drive off, resulting in a loud bang. With luck, the pad material won't have parted from the back plate! Surface rust on the discs usually clears quickly, whilst heavy corrosion requires replacement.

Straight six engines are especially reliable when used regularly.

Fluids
Old, acidic oil can corrode bearings. Uninhibited coolant can corrode internal waterways. Lack of antifreeze can cause the core plug to be pushed out, or even cracks in the block or head. Silt settling and solidifying can cause overheating.

Brake fluid absorbs water from the atmosphere and should be renewed every two years. Old fluid with a high water content can cause corrosion and pistons/callipers/bleed nipples to seize, and can cause brake failure when the water boils near hot braking components.

Tyre sidewall bulge.

Tyre problems
Tyres that have supported the weight of the car in a single position for some time develop flat spots, resulting in some (usually temporary) vibration. They lose pressure over time, too. The tyre walls may have cracks or (blister-type) bulges, meaning new tyres are needed. Even if the tyres appear fine, replacement of old ones on a sports car like a Z4 is recommended, as the rubber loses grip with time.

Shock absorbers (dampers)

With lack of use, the dampers lose their elasticity, leak, or even seize. Creaking, groaning and stiff suspension are signs of this problem.

Rubber and plastic

Radiator hoses may have perished and split, possibly resulting in the loss of all coolant. Window and door seals can harden and leak. Gaiters/boots can crack. Wiper blades harden.

Electrics

The battery will be of little use if it has not been charged for many months. Earthing/grounding problems are common when the connections have corroded. Sparkplug electrodes often corrode in an unused engine. Wiring insulation can harden and fail.

Rotting exhaust system

Cars idling in the garage rarely get hot enough to burn off the moisture in the exhaust. Exhaust gas contains a high water content, and although all Z4s have a stainless steel system as standard, it is likely the exhaust clamps and bolts would corrode.

Split ARB drop link boot.

Stainless steel exhaust as standard.

16 The Community
– key people, organisations and companies in the Z4 world

Part of the ownership appeal is the collective experience of being part of a community of like-minded owners; whether it's a knowing nod or wave when passing another Z4, a chat in a car park or petrol station or a club meeting. The level of participation is purely down to you but I can certainly recommend you get along to at least one organised event, to see how you find it.

Clubs
Many countries have a BMW affiliated national club, with different regions, model specific registers and well organised national events. In addition, club membership often brings genuinely useful discounts on parts and insurance, and a printed and digital magazine.

Trackdays
Every Z4, regardless of model, is capable of being driven on track – I urge you to consider it. These trackdays/

Club meetings take place regularly.

HPDE are non-competitive, fun events that take place on race circuits all over the world, where you drive your own car without speed limits, pedestrians or oncoming traffic! Qualified instructors will help you drive safely and get the best out of your Z4, and the lessons learned here make you a better and safer driver on the road.

Accidents are very rare, and track specific insurance is available if you prefer. Providing your car has been recently serviced and you restrict the length of your sessions to just a few laps at a time, with a warm up and cool down lap each side of your hot laps, reliability throughout the day should be fine. In more than 200 track events in various cars I have experienced just two failures (and no accidents); neither were in a BMW, I might add, and both times they were faults that would have occurred on the road anyway.

The author in a Z4M
Roadster at Laguna Seca.
(Courtesy Dito Milian/gotbluemilk.com)

Social media
Z4 enthusiast groups have sprung up all over the world, sharing photos, experiences and parts for sale instantly. They are not so good for detailed technical help, however, with older discussions rapidly disappearing and a limited search facility.

Website forums

Whilst web forums are not as widely used as they once were (due to the popularity of other forms of social media), they are still a superb resource of information and way of finding out about local gatherings. With thousands of people owning and writing about the Z4, it is safe to say that no matter what the question someone has probably asked and answered it before, so make full use of the forums' search facilities. Many owners have written 'how to' guides with step by step instructions to guide you through a variety of DIY jobs, from simply changing the oil through to full engine rebuilds. The following are just some of the sites available:
z4-forum.com
zroadster.org
zpost.com

Tuning and modifying

As many suspension systems, brakes and engines are shared with the E46, there is an abundance of tuning parts and companies that can improve or change characteristics of your car. Even the briefest of online searches brings up a wealth of knowledge on changing styling or increasing the performance of your Z4, with brands including KW, Bilstein, ACSchnitzer, Alpina, Shrick, AP, ESS, VAC, Birds and Evolve to name just a few.

The Eventuri carbon induction kit produces a superb sound.

Software from Carly, INPA and NCS Expert allow users to change certain functions on the Z4, such as keyfob button functions, follow-me-home lights, Mtrack handling, and so much more.

Manuals, how to

At the time of writing there is no specific commercial Z4 guide tailored to the home mechanic, although Haynes covers certain parts of the oily bits in its E46 3 Series book:

E86 aftermarket lip spoiler.

Haynes Repair Manual BMW 3 Series 1999-2006 and Z4 Models (03-05), Robert Maddox, ISBN 9781563925986.
eBay offers workshop CDs that include wiring diagrams.

Other books

There are surprisingly few books on the Z4. The best of them is:
BMW Z3 and Z4 – The Complete Story, James Taylor, ISBN 9781785002762

17 Vital statistics
– essential data at your fingertips

Pre-face-lift
E85 2-litre Roadster N46B20 four-cylinder 16v 148bhp
E85 2.2-litre Roadster M54B22 six-cylinder 24v 168bhp
E85 2.5-litre Roadster M54B25 six-cylinder 24v 192bhp
E85 3-litre Roadster M54B30 six-cylinder 24v 230bhp
Alpina Roadster S 3.4-litre M52/B3 six-cylinder 24v 300bhp

Post 2006 face-lift
E85 2-litre Roadster N46B20 four-cylinder 16v 148bhp
E85 2.5i Roadster N52B25 six-cylinder 24v 177bhp
E85 2.5si Roadster N52B25 six-cylinder 24v 215bhp
E85 3.0i Roadster N52B30 six-cylinder 24v 215bhp (USA only)
E85 + E86 3.0si N52B30 six-cylinder 24v 261bhp
E85M + E86M 3.2 S54B32 six-cylinder 24v 338bhp

A selection of Roadster performance figures as a guide

Capacity	BHP	Torque	0-60mph	Max speed	Weight
2-litre	148bhp@6200rpm	148lb ft@3600rpm	8.2sec	137mph	1225kg
3-litre	231bhp@5900rpm	221lb ft@3500rpm	5.7sec	155mph ltd	1290kg
3-litre SSG semiauto	231bhp@5900rpm	221lb ft@3500rpm	5.7sec	155mph ltd	1290kg
3-litre Steptronic auto	231bhp@5900rpm	221lb ft@3500rpm	6sec	151mph	1290kg
3-litre	261bhp@6600rpm	232lb ft@2750rpm	5.5sec	155mph ltd	1310kg
3.4-litre	300bhp@6300rpm	266lb ft@4800rpm	5.1sec	169mph	1320kg
3.2-litre	338bhp@7900rpm	269lb ft@4900rpm	4.7sec	155mph ltd	1450kg

Total production: 180856 Roadsters, 17094 Coupés, 197950 Z4s in total.

Dimensions
Length: 4090mm (161in)
Width: 1780mm (70.1in) including
  mirrors 1904mm (75in)
Height: E85 – 1299mm (51.1in); E86 –
  1268mm (49.9in)
Fuel tank: 55 litres (12 imperial gallons)
Turning circle: 9m (29.5ft)

**Face-lift 3-litre Si Roadster with 224
alloys. (Courtesy Colin McMorran)**

The Essential Buyer's Guide™ series ...

Also from Veloce –

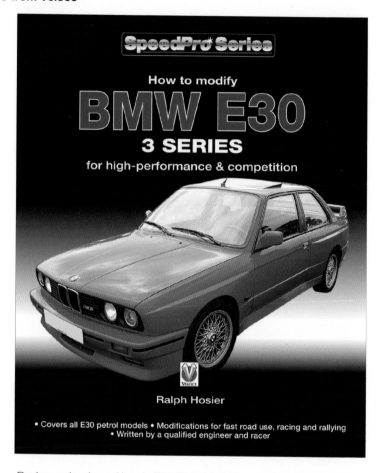

Buying a classic and iconic E30 BMW 3 Series can be just the start of a wonderful adventure. This book explains how these fantastic cars can be modified to suit a vast range of applications, from fast road use to race and rally..

ISBN: 978-1-845844-38-7
Paperback • 25x20.7cm • 128 pages • 536 colour and b&w pictures

For more information and price details, visit our website at www.veloce.co.uk
• email: info@veloce.co.uk • Tel: +44(0)1305 260068
* prices subject to change, p&p extra

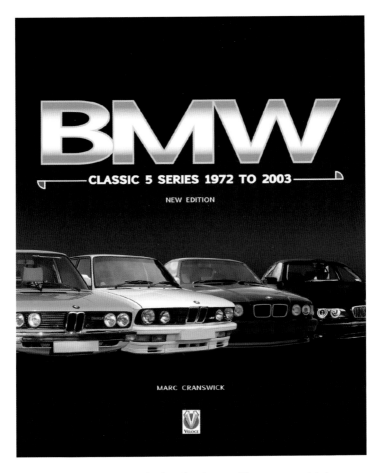

A look at BMW's 5 series in the classic era. Observes model changes
and development from 1972, to the end of e39 5 series production.
Complete descriptions and pictures of BMW Motorsport cars, plus
the exotic tuner specials from Germany. BMW's rise in business
internationally is also examined.

ISBN: 978-1-787110-61-8
Hardback • 25x20.7cm • 232 pages • 250 pictures

Index